MUSE FOUND IN A COLONIZED BODY

Muse

Found in a

Colonized Body

POEMS

YESENIA MONTILLA

FOUR WAY BOOKS
TRIBECA

LIBRARY OF CONGRESS CATALOGING-IN-PUBLICATION DATA
Names: Montilla, Yesenia, author.
Title: Muse found in a colonized body / Yesenia Montilla.
Description: [New York] : [Four Way Books], [2022]
Identifiers: LCCN 2022003865 | ISBN 9781954245327 (paperback) | ISBN
  9781954245419 (epub)
Subjects: LCGFT: Poetry.
Classification: LCC PS3613.O54895 M87 2022 | DDC 811/.6--dc23/eng/20220128
LC record available at https://lccn.loc.gov/2022003865
This book is manufactured in the United States of America and printed on
acid-free paper.

Four Way Books is a not-for-profit literary press. We are grateful for the assistance
we receive from individual donors, public arts agencies, and private foundations
including the NEA, NEA Cares, Literary Arts Emergency Fund, and the
New York State Council on the Arts, a state agency.

We are a proud member of the Community of Literary Magazines and Presses.

"There is not occupation of territory on the one hand and independence of persons on the other. It is the country as a whole, its history, its daily pulsation that are contested, disfigured, in the hope of a final destruction. Under these conditions, the individual's breathing is an observed, an occupied breathing. It is a combat breathing."

FRANTZ FANON

A Dying Colonialism

"Freeing yourself was one thing, claiming ownership of that freed self was another."

TONI MORRISON

Beloved

"Poetry is an act of witness. It is also an act of evidence."

KHALED MATTAWA

"We must always be disturbed by the truth."

DŌGEN ZENJI

For Us

CONTENTS

MUSE FOUND IN A COLONIZED BODY

MUSE FOUND IN A COLONIZED BODY

There is no greater love than the love a wolf feels

for the lamb it doesn't eat

HÉLÈNE CIXOUS

I.

They say when the Spaniards came we thought them
gods. They came with sincere eyes, but insincere
mouths & cocks they knew something about the
universe & we only knew about the earth, not
about the stars unless being guided by them is
a kind of knowing, but no, in those days the stars
knew us more than we them. & that might be the
difference between the wolf & the lamb, our
relationship to bounty. I think what I want
to say here is that to the wolf go the spoils & yet
there is something about being a lamb—the danger
the never knowing when the wolf will be hungry enough.
How do you not love yourself when you constantly
survive your undoing just by being precious?
I don't like coyness, if I love you I will take your mouth
first because that is where the breath lives, does that
make me a wolf, or does this: when I am near you
I shackle my intentions & feasts with my eyes, I won't
dare eat of your flesh. How could I? It would be like
the snake that eats itself from the tail, eventually it
chokes on everything, its rough scales, its heart all
colonized & tender, the whole world becomes its
body half-eaten & dragging in the dirt—

Manifest Destiny

How we took something
like universal law & made it
violent. How we are violent.
How we think destiny is two
things: a reward & a good
time. How we think manifest
is one thing: a destiny. How
we don't know how to be still.
How we don't know how to
desire & then let go. How we
want it all, only to be less than
tender with it. How when spring
time comes around, we find
ourselves in a field surrounded
by dandelions & when a soft wind
blows the specs stir & take flight
around us. How we know nothing,
so we call it   snow—

Maps

For Marcelo

Some maps have blue borders
like the blue of your name
or the tributary lacing of
veins running through your
father's hands. & how the last
time I saw you, you held
me for so long I saw whole
lifetimes flooding by me
small tentacles reaching
for both our faces. I wish
maps would be without
borders & that we belonged
to no one & to everyone
at once, what a world that
would be. Or not a world
maybe we would call it
something more intrinsic
like forgiving or something
simplistic like river or dirt.
& if I were to see you
tomorrow & everyone you
came from had disappeared
I would weep with you & drown
out any black lines that this
earth allowed us to give it—
because what is a map but
a useless prison? We are all

so lost & no naming of blank
spaces can save us. & what

is a map but the delusion of
safety? The line drawn is always
in the sand & folds on itself
before we're done making it.
& that line, there, south of
el rio, how it dares to cover
up the bodies, as though we
would forget who died there
& for what? As if we could
forget that if you spin a globe
& stop it with your finger
you'll land it on top of someone
living, someone who was not
expecting to be crushed by thirst.

Some Notes on Being Human

The dead are   everywhere
The mouse rotting away inside my walls
The rat in the basement trap
& just yesterday, my Dominican cab driver
ran over a pigeon on the corner of 145th & St. Nick

I am used to that
It's the dead people I can't handle
So many   & I fear we all have our hands
in it

& can I mention circles?
How the universe is made up of them
yet we behave so linear, as if life weren't
a round mouth full of reverie, as if stirring
the pot or our morning Bustelo wasn't a
circular action

Everything is a spiral, as improbable as a galaxy
as destructive as a hurricane

& this is just to say that there are more solar systems
than there are us
& we still haven't learned to live
as stars

& while we are on the subject of living
is this all there is to it?

To be born
To become enraged
To break ourselves against an indestructible
machine
But what about being a
blinding beautiful & incorruptible thing?

& speaking of corruption
have I mentioned   Colonization?
Being imposed a foster parent without
arms to hold you   only   teeth & spit

& did I mention Africa
Or does that require another poem?

I once had a lover that told me:
You're sooooooo   Black
I took it as a compliment
He meant it as
Goodbye

Every Sunday I call my abuela
& we go over all the week's tragedies
She is brown & woman
trauma is the only way she stays tethered
to the earth.

She tells me ponte las pilas
& for hours I search my body for slots

where batteries might fit

because I imagine the only way to save humanity

is to be a little less   human

Invasion Prevention

          The next time I let tongues
roam my body whose ancestors never knew   Lucumí
Yoruba, Taíno, or another Arawakan spilling out their mouth
    let my past me   remember
that a white man never asked me for
        anything that
he didn't assume was already his—& ain't that
the last of the learning I need to do before
          leaving this earth

Just yesterday I saw one flower peeking through cold dirt
& I realized spring was here—

MUSE FOUND IN A COLONIZED BODY

II.

Far in the future
another earth even
if we haven't gone
the way of Christina's
dinosaur ghost
if we haven't invested
billions in trying to own
the exact light
found in a firefly's
laughter—We will look
back on one of the great
plagues of the 21st century
as just   loneliness—

Eartha Kitt as Muse

The eyes are two saucers filled with every
        forlorn woman's last meal: roasted
        chicken & a good Bordeaux   & how
the heart is found in the neck's thick artery, ready
            for a man's good touch.

Eartha, I know nothing about fame or fortune
        but I know a little about being so lonely

that even the peony's elaborate bloom cannot keep me company.
You're so damn pretty, that I could write a poem about you
        & you
        & (insert lover's name)   We both have had plenty
to spare   & darling, I love how

we look in the mirror & kiss the air

       & how when our hand waves in greeting
the sky & all its particles dance & a sweet sigh
escapes from our parted lips
       & isn't that sound a kind of tenderness?

How laughter bolts from our mouths like a wild
heart drumming

this is how we muzzle the world—

A Poem with Birds in It

The universe has many mysteries
& we being each our own universe
we are full of blossoms
The oak tree's secret song
The mycelium network like a million
silkworm threads swinging underfoot
There is a cleaning the body does
if you have a good healer
There is a reverie in being
when you have a good teacher
There is a bounty in fully living
Please believe me
The earth begs us to call it our lover
& our body its house
& our mouth its nightingale
If you sit super still during the summer solstice
you'll see a thousand flocks take flight into
        the dusty sky
It will sound like a humming caught in the throat
It will feel like a needle strumming
It will vibrate everything & just when you think
you do not deserve such beauty
      —you'll grow wings

All Barns Are Red Because of Dying Stars

The iron(y) of stars, lonely & on their deathbeds, being responsible
for the color of barns. & how this should be its own kind of table
full of elements that we've never been able to fully realize peace
or (brother)hood. & I am sitting here, trying to remember if I've
ever seen a barn any other color but the color of dying things, or
if I would ever want to bask in the slow temperament of a blue
barn with its cool lulling song or a kind of green that reminds me
of a spruce or freshly cut grass. In the dead of night, I imagine
a star whirling its way to earth, weeping as its light goes out. Landing
in a field somewhere in upstate New York or nowhere Idaho
& becoming a barn, living out its afterlife bloodied & hollow. What a
simple way for such a god to retire, if only all of us could die out
this way, protecting cows, horses—

How to Greet a Warbler

for Christian Cooper

Today, walking in the tall grass
close to home, mask on, ears wide
I spotted a warbler all yellow-bellied
with its human eyes & soft-tongued
song & I imagined how we could have
lost another one of us to the kind of
violence only whiteness is allowed to
dream up & enact. His wings were

rousing up dirt in protest as if he too
was envisioning loss & I swear I wanted
to kneel before him & make of him
        a church—

Philando Castile's Name Is So Beautiful
I Remember Love Making

You are no longer as beautiful
as you once were,
neither am I it is a symptom
of longing or losing—to lose
your hair or fill out
in the wrong places

We lost the small
window of time where both
our bodies could've been naked
in bed petitioning poetry
to save us & now all we have
is the starkness of Black
bodies lying everywhere
on roadsides,

in the car,
outside the bodega,
near the docks

When I first heard his name
I remember thinking—
Philando Castile,
he's a prince
or a god, or just a man
riding in his car with child
& love in tow.

Or a moan in my mouth,
or the spider in Nikki Giovanni's poem.
Or just the beast in every white man's imagination,
with horns & teeth & a gun for a hand—

In this dead world
full of the dying
I no longer care about losing my
dress or my heart.

I only care about revolution
& the ugly business of revenge.

Between the knife handle & its blade,
that is the only home I know
that gives true pleasure—

Muse: Judge

Sheila Abdus-Salaam did not
kill herself. How could she?
She ain't a star that just
decides one day to die out,
she was a planet & some asteroid
knocked her off orbit, turned her
into another dead Black woman.

The news feeds us the possibilities
of what they know which is a kind of
whiteness that imagines Black women
killing themselves in jail cells & public
parks or a kind of world where Black girls
disappear from their neighborhoods
only to pop up later having joined
the circus or a cult.

Whiteness thinks Blackness is whiteness.
Whiteness thinks we the same. & how
could we be? We be the starved,
the overlooked, the myth whiteness
makes up to feel better about their
place in things—& sometimes we're
too loud & sometimes they decide we
gotta go, & when we are murdered we are
like a tree, no one around to hear us
fall

Listen, a judge died, she was Black,
let that not be a noiseless death,
let it be earsplitting, let it be thunderous—

A Perfect Game

To this day I still remember sitting
on my abuelo's lap watching   the Yankees hit,
    then run, a soft wind rounding the bases
every foot tap to the white pad gentle as a   kiss.

How I loved those afternoons languidly
    eating jamón sandwiches & drinking root beer.

Later, when I knew something about   the blue collar
man—my father who worked with his hands & tumbled
    into the house exhausted like heat in a rainstorm—
        I became a Mets fan.

Something about   their unclean   faces
                their mustaches seemed rough
to the touch. They had names like   Wally & Dykstra.
I was certain I would   marry a man just like them

        that is until   Sammy Sosa came along

with his smile a reptile that only knew about laying in the sun.
His arms where canons & his skin burnt cinnamon
        that glistened in my dreams.

Everyone said he was not beautiful.
Out in the streets where the men set up shop playing dominoes
I'd hear them say between the yelling of   capicú
        "como juega, pero feo como el diablo."

I knew nothing of my history
        of the in-fighting on an island in which one side swore
it was only one thing: pallid, pristine.   & I didn't know
        that Sammy carried this history like a   tattoo.

That he wished every day to be   *white*.

It is a perfect game this race war, it is everywhere,   living
        in the American bayou as much as
        the Dominican dirt roads.
It makes a man do something to his skin that seems unholy.
It makes that same man change   eye color like a soft
        summer dress slipped on slowly.
It makes a grandmother ask her granddaughter

                if she's suffering
        from something feverish
because that could be the only excuse why
        her hair has not been straightened
like a ballerina's back   dyed the color of wild
        daffodils growing in an outfield.

Sammy hit 66 home runs one year
                & that was still   not   enough
        to make him feel handsome

or worthy of that Blackness that I believe a gift
even today while Black churches burn & Black bodies
disappear from one day to the next the same as old
pennies

I think of him often   barely remember what he looked like
        but I can recall his   hunched shoulders in the
dug out   his perfect swing
          & how maybe   he spit out   something black
from his mouth   after every   single   strike—

MUSE FOUND IN A COLONIZED BODY

III.

Trauma is inherited
They built a country on trauma
A country with a death wish
A mad country

Some days
    I want to swallow a million stars
    spit them out
        start over—

Muse Found in South Carolina

*

Unarmed Black man shot   *again*
                & it took me a moment to swallow
                        :: officer charged with   murder ::

Because gravity is still working just fine & it ain't the end of the world
                birds are still chirping as if nothing's gone wrong for a white man
                        & I wanna holler *hallelujah!*

Celebrating in my bed with champagne &
                slow whistles escaping through my teeth

maybe I shouldn't be all fucking uppity about it
maybe I shouldn't celebrate   reprimand
                a Black man is still dead   *again*

**

Lately I am a slow burning bourbon in the throat
horrified at my own bitterness
I am going to build a shrine
with my soot-filled heart
to a hero in this story

                                Feidin
sauntering about being canopied from the sun by trees without eyes—
I won't forget your name I will always remember   you

recording a Black man   running   away
& getting
shot
in the back
thank you for staying & capturing humanity   at its worst

***

& to the grass
thank you for how you cradled   Walter's body
    & soaked up   his final heaving breaths—

Making Love to Captain America

Sometimes I want to punch you in your perfect teeth

TONY STARK

Could any human be more perfect?
He's all the pretty whiteness I was taught to want to
be or to have or to seduce maybe
with my taínafrican roots, my dusting of europa
found in the D codon of my DNA somewhere near
the kink of my hair & size of my breasts—

I am not sure how I love him more
with his uniform off or on
with the shield in front of him to ward off the enemy
or with his shield behind his back
his arms left open for an embrace

He's always right, even when he's wrong, even when
he doesn't know the difference between the mouth open
for exit, or for entry

I want to make love to him

Be wrapped up in all the stars & stripes of his convictions
I want to point out to him that the enemy is not always out there
Sometimes your enemy is your neighbor
Sometimes your enemy is some kid from Queens with daddy issues
Sometimes your enemy runs for president on your soil & calls you a thief
a rapist, a criminal, a choke in America's throat

Sometimes the enemy is forgetting that Cap & I can never see eye to eye
because he's been on ice so long he doesn't know

that America has become a dirty word that I only still use out of habit
That the habit is a secret thing I don't mention like my deep desire
for white boys & my constant need to break my body against them

Evolution has been unkind, Cap

Did you learn anything while you were cold?
Say yes & maybe there's hope for us all
Maybe we should all be put on ice too

Or maybe we should just let you loose
Will you destroy my enemies as easily as you do your own?
I don't want to know

The fantasy of you is so sweet
let me stay sleeping
let me stay dreaming
& when I wake let me roll over
& see your face, pretty white boy
with pretty teeth, if I punch you
I am the only one that bleeds—

To Cast[1]

*

The question is always posed at a party
    If you were a cast away on a deserted island
        who would you want to   hold?

& the penny is hurled in the air
we are for eternity torn between a face   & a tail—

& we fall into one of two categories
      those who cast spells   & those that cast things aside

love may not be discarded but shipwrecked yes
& so on—

**

I've only been fly fishing once   it is something quite stunning
      the way the string dances above your head like wild imaginings
the striking of nylon against the pebbled water

the lure with its many colors dangling just above the wake
glistening like booty & the fish come   if you're silent

knee deep in Oshun's river :: rubber against the skin :: lips slack from trying

***

I want to hold   *you—*
If tomorrow the lush green of an island were my only dress
It'd be   *you—*

****

I am about to cast a   vote
              & I might die anyway
                              regardless of the outcome—

1. to throw or hurl, fling :: to throw off or away :: to direct (the eye, a glance, etc), especially in cursory manner :: to cause to fall upon something or in certain directions; send forth :: to draw, as in telling fortunes :: to throw out (a fishing line, net, bait, etc.) :: to fish in (a stream, an area, etc.) :: to throw down or bring to the ground—

To Pimp a Butterfly as Muse

I want to honor the caterpillar's made-it-to-26-years-old swag

    & the locusts how they descend   on everything
    even my metaphor(s)

Let me start over   things fall apart   & I am

finally over my white boy stage
my apologies, I am a slow learner

I've never seen a butterfly chase a cow
boy, why did I?
Living in this kill a mockingbird world while butterflies
are made to hoe stroll
I might die from this double consciousness

Listening to Lamar
his Midori Sour of a voice
echoing   like a priest
or a lover that can last   hours

I daydream of
    his rap   tongue
    how it seduces
    how it cleaves to my big girl waist
    how it fucks everyone into a remarkable rousing
    how he holds us with his stiff grip, asking

Is there any justice left in this world?

Dissent these days is so hushed   voiceless even
        You could hear a Black Lives Matter button plummet
        into the abyss   never to be imagined   again—

MUSE FOUND IN A COLONIZED BODY

IV.

Before the bees   nothing
          like before free labor   nothing neither
I think what I mean is that before I learned about
                    pollination,   love,
the discovering of   another to make
          something sweet I already knew
about the things   my body could   do
          without compensation—

Karl Marx as Muse

I am no Jenny; but I want you to write me a love poem
Something about a proletariat uprising
Something about free water & food
Something about more than just survival

You've whispered in my ear a dozen times:
you write poems because of a delicate fissure
in the ruling class's ideology. & when I look
at my paycheck, for a moment I feel very
bourgeoisie, all petticoats & pale skin.

But later,   after I've paid everything
                    after I've watched the Kardashians on E!
                    after another bottle of malbec gone

I dream of setting the world on fire—
I dream of you & your precious beard   how if alive now

we wouldn't be friends, you'd live in Brooklyn & we'd call you a hipster
          sitting in shadowy bars
drinking bourbon & discussing your own theories   but never
writing them down   never that—

Oh, precious Karl, friend of all things revolutionary

take me to bed   tell me something about alienation that you haven't already

If I stare too hard at the world it all becomes an assembly line

Lover, I beg you   gift me a revolution—

Up on My Bougie Ass Shit

The brie cheese priced at $30/lb
The face cream that promises to drop 5 years
The yoga class that suspends you in mid air
The forearm tattoo with blackbirds
The septum ring with emeralds
The mattress that regulates your temperature
The Spanish ham made from happy pigs
The cashmere throw that doubles as a scarf
The bottle of wine for special occasions
     let me bathe in it—
The body massage that uses hot stones
The infrared sauna that melts fat fast
The first class seat   to Paris

               to Dubai

               to Cape Town

               to Seychelles

               to Bali

               to Maldives

Sometimes I be up on that bougie ass shit
A full moon is just another way for me to shift the tides
A sunny day a vault full of vitamin D

I want to get paid to do kegels with my yoni egg in a king
size bed after my vajacial while everyone watches—

I have big dreams   for big
things

Some days I can't stand myself I am so pretentious
Some days I fill my Anthropologie cart to the brim
                & then delete
Some days   I can taste the caviar on my tongue
                I can feel the feathers in the bed
                I can drag my lips across a gold bowl
                     full of manuka honey
& quiver from the extravagance of it all

Some days   I say dinner at Per Se   I deserve it
Some days   I am made of glitter   I explode—

Muse Found in LES

Something about Avenues A through D with their gaze on me all fishnet stocking like holey & holy. & the way that if I turn on just the right corner I'll find myself falling for a long-haired dude with a pretty mouth & a surgeon's hands. & I still remember that one night, coming out of Nuyo how the 6'3" Lady Gaga look alike grabbed my hand & serenaded me. So we walked to Orchard & sat in the Taqueria for hours eating guac & drinking margaritas talking shit about all the men whose hearts we'd broken. & we wished that Katja had not been so crowded because we really wanted a pretzel with cheese & to share a sizzling sausage plate & for a moment nothing else mattered except our frantic longing for goo & salt & someone's hot skin on ours—

Chasing Duende

After Natalie

They say he has a lover's tongue
all warm liquid & plated fur. That
when he decides to lick you like
the rim of a salted glass the
moon becomes full behind your
eyelids & god stays at bay. Querido
Duende I've worshipped you, you
without a face, your irrational heart. I say
ven a mi & I get my monthly blood.
My pockets are full of coins now
I use them to pay the ferryman
I shuttle the dead across the river
hold their hand as though they
were my children. Grandfather
& your tribe of thousands.
Grandmother, could I have birthed
you? Made you in your most perfect
image all blue-eyed & thin-lipped? Sister,
not your time. Father, any day now.
Last night I dreamt of hands on me
not like divination but like devotion
two cocks & a naked neck in the yard.
Yemaya tells me: sacrifice them, all of
them, pluck their feathers & bring
your honey mouth to the shore. She
likes sweet & soft things. Forces me
to tell the story of my great love,

but love is an endangered word,
untranslatable, its etymology closer
to that of raven or he who won't
let me touch him—What if my wrists
bleed from such longing? What if I choke
on a picture? What if I forget the thinness
of my waist at dawn & lose myself
to magic? What then? Will I ever recover?
Will the monster that hides in the soles
of my shoes finally reveal himself? Will
he be she, or they, or a god with red lipstick?
I swear I hear whispering in the bed
sheets & my eyes grow heavy, my hips
start to rock, a valley between two mounds
at the very beginning; before light, before the
rib was plucked & the honeybee knelt at
the flowers entryway. Yemaya, will you
bring me Duende, bring me a lock of his
hair, his head severed that I can sew
onto me like a new dress? Duende, do I know
your half-eaten smile, your dirty words?
Have we already met & I confused your
sucking for a song, this heartache for
a poem? When I was kissed by the full
lipped girl at midnight I saw another's
face & I haven't been able to see anything
else. Brown eyes, crooked teeth, a beard
so manicured, like a rich man's lawn—

Searching for My Own Body

Which is to say that like a good theoretical objectified body, my identity was
created not by me but by the various desires and beliefs of those around me

DANIEL BORZUTZKY

My body is a small   cave door
it's a slick whale   a jubilant
sea of tall grass that sways
& makes its way across   countries
& lovers   I love   love-making
I don't remember a time when
I wasn't interested in touch
I have these   breasts
& some would want to come
on hands & knees to worship   them
call me flower   or   desert
Maybe I was only supposed to be
stone or   a baby eel
long & layered   a   nun?
I don't remember ever   saying
                         yes or no
I am searching   for my own   body
not the one I was told is so
I want to be always   open
                              like a canyon
Maybe I was only supposed to be
tree or temple   In some circles I am
just an open gate   a   sinful bauble
Once someone said   you are *this*
& I never   questioned it

40

So   when I place hand ·   on face or thigh
the direction is always   north
lay me down
I like contact   I search my own body
for   God   or someone like   her—

Masturbating to a G

because I never met a light-skinned brother I didn't want to drown in
                 & my hands how they are made for riding
El DeBarge's voice a slow simmer in my gut; having spent days
without my bed
without an avalanche in my throat
so I am ready for remedy
my fingers spread to pry open
& El's face   like a thief of things
          like a voyeur on voyage

smile wide as the hole I bury my heart in
teeth bright like my grandmother's good china
his eyes cavernous like that time in Italy
where the grotto plucked me from the sea

& I want to say *shoot outta here* as though he were
                    an ex heartbreak
& I also want to let him watch me, wildly come
                    to the conclusion of it all
as I quickly realize it's not about this man
            but another

where is my love croons through & it is 1995
Washington DC
the sky purple from all the bruising
& just like that my greatest love is dead
& just like that I've stolen Pat's line
& just like that I am aching from the loss of it

& just like that every man is El DeBarge
                    & El DeBarge is—

my body bucks with violence
because pleasure is the kind of throbbing
no loss can contain
because I've never trusted a Black man
                    to stay alive—

& yet still, here, 20 years later
I am in awe of the body
how it can still find   joy
while being picked at
by a murder
               of gulls—

MUSE FOUND IN A COLONIZED BODY

V.

Last night a mosquito
murmured in my ear
something about forgiveness
& then she bit me—

The natural world is a distorted
image on a machete's smooth
blade & I am in it. How could
I not be when my heart is a

fat flute or a round harmonica?
I want to say that it will all be
okay, that the storm is just an
indicator of natural selection

but what if I don't survive?
What if I am already extinct
& don't even know it? How
do I reconcile all this wine

with water? How do I save
my pen & notebook too?
When there are choices, the
earth will tilt slant to rouse us

The honeybees are dying
& the grains are all GMO

We ruin everything. &
we still beg for beauty—

Hamilton Heights Starbucks

Been waiting for a Hamilton Heights Starbucks
for 10 years. Dreaming of Sunday morning papers
& poems while sippin' my triple venti half sweet
non-fat caramel macchiato to the latest coffee house
appropriate tunes. I wanna be a white girl, no cares
just lounging about with hipster black glasses & a cute
but non-threatening boyfriend waiting for me downtown
so we can hit up first Saturdays at the Brooklyn Museum
before an indie concert at the pier at dusk in fall.

I want a world where all those things do not spell gentrification.

Where I don't think about Cornel West being arrested in
Ferguson between my third shot of espresso & my weekly
trip to Whole Foods & for a moment I am seasick, because
Middle Passage is still happening, except now we are being
transported in police vans to prisons made just for us.

No one drinks white mochas but still it stays on the menu.

Last night, I had to bring my eighty-year-old neighbor
my leftovers because these days her foot don't work
too well & her children have forgotten her name
& cat food is just so damn expensive ever since
the C-Town supermarket got themselves an organic section.

In order to wake up each morning, I can't think too hard on this world.

Maybe I should really be careful what I wish for,

that Starbucks is coming whether I wish it so

or not. & did I mention, my 80-year-old neighbor used to be

a concert pianist. She played at Lincoln Center, her whole

life dedicated to her brown elegant fingers touching white—

La Bodega—A Gentrification Story

Outside the bodega it is spring
a 60-degree evening & the men
are playing dominoes. Their
granddaughters with pig tails
& pink bomber jackets & matching
leggings are hopscotching, I take
a turn before going inside—

On the line I hold on to a bag of
perejil, una yautia, dos yucas
y un cartón de huevos. Tonight
dinner is a Taíno feast—& this
is where my mind has wandered
when the white woman slides in
front of me. She slams her diet coke

bag of butter lettuce, box of rice
a roni & a can of tuna on the
counter. El bodeguero looks in
my direction, he knows I carry
inside me the kind of ancestors
that would cut a bitch, but I say
nothing. The air that comes through

the door is so soft like a lover's
sweet hands & I am feeling generous.

You should carry organic eggs, then
I don't have to go to the supermarket
so out of my way. The bodeguero asks:
are you going to buy all my organic

foods if I order them? She responds
yes, me & all my friends. I stop
paying attention, behind the glass
counter are three Dominican
newspapers on display. One
of the captions stops me—

Exclusivo, Quién Era Cristóbal Colón
In an instant I am giggling
uncontrollably. I have no idea
who he was, but I know at the very
least he was the kind of human
that landed in a place some called
paradise & instead of enjoying the view

he asked for organic eggs & cut the line—

When Malcolm Wins the Lottery He Buys Me—

a panda
a vintage bike
pistachio colored
with a bell
& a basket
a mini cooper
red with stripes
& a bike rack
Malcolm wins
the lottery
so I'll build
my own
nation the one
that resides
in my imagination
when Malcolm
wins the lottery
I'll build my own
police force
to keep him safe
safe like the fig tree
on 9th & Christian
in the middle
of Philly
safe like Ara's
stars in the eye
of Neil's telescope
I'll build a bunker

for Black & Brown
bodies to wait
out the end
of the world
If we all go
into hiding
will white
folks kill one
another? This
is the end
is it not? How
can it not be
when a police
officer can slip
his gun out
of his holster
like a tongue
place it to
the back
of a man & pull
the trigger
easier than
a kiss? It has to
be the end
right? I mean
when Malcolm
wins the lottery
I might buy a
time machine
but where could
we go? Where

in time could we
be where we
are all safe & Black
& free?

MUSE FOUND IN A COLONIZED BODY

VI.

Everything I want
becomes something else

This is part of being
a colonized body

What is enough when
enough is not quantifiable?

Naming the Baby

I couldn't bring myself
to read through Breonna's social
media but some say she believed 2020
would be her year. She even
imagined a baby growing steady
in her belly. I imagine her choosing
the baby's name with care. Taking
all the months she had to name it
something like Pearl or V or Cheryl
There are a million baby names
to choose from the good book
but what do you name
the baby that never would be
in the year that should've been
yours? Do you name her
Revolution? Do you name her
A World Screaming? Do you
name her Fire? Let her
burn the house down—

Gut Gravity

For Chadwick & My abuelitos

When we were little, my mom used to
threaten us kids with *an ass-kicking*
that not even Pupo could fix.

& no one knew this Pupo. He resided somewhere
between my imagination & my hopefulness
A man or an octopus. A hot dog vendor near
the corner of 72nd & Central Park West or a magician
who pulled lamp shades out of hats in Avenida
Cienfuegos in my mother's hometown of Holguin, Cuba

& what of the ass-kicking, what of the fixing?
It wasn't till later when I asked my grandmother: *¿abuela quién*
es Pupo? That she explained to me that the mystery man
was a gastroenterologist in Havana, that he cared
for my great-grandmother when the cancer *back there*
consumed her, that because of him she lived an extra
3 years past her expiration date. Pupo was a proper ass doctor
& he had folklore status among our people.

Memory is a juggernaut: today I think of Pupo
how desperately I needed him in '99 when
the cancer back there took my mother's father
or in '16 when it took my father's father
his small hole had become a gaping one you could
                                        see through—a window

All this to say
　　　　the colon is a galaxy
made of stars　　　　　　that can go
　　　　　　supernova
& destroy us like a big bang or kill us slowly, methodically even
while it dares us to create a legacy in 3 year, 2 years, 1—

Wakanda Forever—all that Vibranium, but what we needed
　　　　　　　was a Pupo
　　　　　　　　　　for the king—

At 38 I had my first colonoscopy, I remember two things:

The ass doctor was beautiful, the kind of man
　　　　only Hollywood makes & I couldn't remember
　　　　　　if my Brazilian had also included an ass wax

After, when he went over my chart he said: it was all clear
　　you have one of the most beautiful colons I've ever seen
　　& I remember blushing as if he'd said
　　I were　　　beautiful
　　　　& in that moment

I was, because in my family
　　　　a beautiful colon is infinite
time:　　　　　a faceless clock
　　a gut full of light　　constellations
　　　　　　gravity—

MUSE FOUND IN A COLONIZED BODY

VII.

Let's suspend the belief that equality exists
even in love, like there's no such thing as equality,
not in a bed.

Listen, I tell you this is a condition of being a colonized
body—we know nothing else but to be occupied

I want to be more than what I know. I want to be
       the caretaker of lovely things—

but trauma is inherited & taking
                is all I know—

Feel Gray, Must Exit

nowhere to go
        but you have to   go   somewhere

if I had a garage I'd have a sale: EVERYTHING MUST GO

even the garage—

my obsession with teeth would prompt me to keep my toothbrush.

       & my ovaries, how they cry lately, maybe I'll leave
my birth control pills behind   make love

to a wanderlust with a wild beard   &
    a sweater like moth fodder   our baby

will look & sound like Iggy Pop
                 born with eyeliner on.

      & I'll never come back   not even for funerals
                   not even if they bought me a ticket—

Letting Go

During meditation this morning
Oprah tells me to dream it & let
go. Dream it & send it to the universe.

She doesn't know that I hold on
to my dreams as if they were lovers

hold on way past the expiration date
way past the signifier for loosen
your grip; eons after the thing I loved
most is dead in my hands. I wanna say

to Oprah: What if the universe wants
to keep the things I want for itself?

The Chiffon dress mustard colored
dreaming. The hummingbird's wings
buzzing as fast as my poet's mind; its
bird face with its human eyelashes

flirting with all my wanting—Oprah,
what if the universe keeps my beach
house? My yogi body? My late nights
kissing Halle & Michael B equally?

What if I have dreamt so big that
the universe thinks I am too small for
such musings? My hands become

wine goblets pouring out rainwater
pouring out desire like ten thousand
meteors flashing in the sky. There,

look there, somewhere between this
constellation & that, every poem I've
ever written, in the universe's library
undiscovered & weeping in the dark—

Confession

If I knew back then that I'd one day be a poet
that one day my words would matter
that one day I might mean something to someone
I might not have had that abortion in '93. Or maybe
I would have, but under a different name. Anne
Sexton taught me everything about lust & shame
but nothing about regret. No matter, when they ask
me why I did it, I'll tell them I was young
& I desperately wanted the fruit to fall far
from the tree, that is to say, my mother's face
is a red stone & I wanted to be a diamond—

Elegy

For Gabo

The world is an ocean in mourning
       drought & dirt covering every starfish

Tell me that I will see you again, that life like love
is not a thruway but a road kinked, entwined;
       my hair in the morning, or a slinky dragging its steel body

I was waiting for you to write me another love story
Love in the time of _____
       capitalism, white privilege, Trump—

Viejo, to me you were a million
lovers, handing me all their pretty
       pennies & I pocketed them in my best dresses.

They scattered you
across a whole field of acorns & they soaked
       you up like a tender breath

Tell me that I will see you again, that on the other
side you will be my greatest love, as you were here
       I need to know that there is always something left—

I am waiting for you to tell me this poem is cliché
but what is cliché but a thousand archetypes making love
       & whispering the same soot & glimmer in one another's ears

Viejo, tell me about your death day, I am waiting to hear about the firing squad

What did you see during your last exhale? Was it many rooms,

your heart's chambers pleading for an open door?

MUSE FOUND IN A COLONIZED BODY

VIII.

Even though there are things
I can't let go of—your smile
at high noon, or the way you
would stare into my body, as
though I housed a whole
country there. & what's
a country in a body except a
colony? & colonization can
happen to a heart as well
as a whole people. & people
seem to overlook that love is
not a freight truck that runs
over the worst parts of us;
it is a bird watcher, face
stretched out towards heaven
waiting to spot wings. & what
do I know about heaven? The
same thing I know about wings,
I can't have it—

Complicated Muse

Last night I could've sworn I time traveled
not forward or back, but askew & slanted
It's my new superpower, how I move
through the world, never in a straight line

I want to know everything about myself
so I spend hours asking the hard questions
What city do you really belong in?
What goddess are you?
What mythical creature do you most resemble?
How many days would you survive in a zombie apocalypse?
How do you   love?

Imaginings are wasteful

            How we invest in them &

                        eventually we will break a mirror

or spill salt   & all the reverie will be for naught

      I want a muse with fishnet abs   that can double

as a dream catcher or a mesh for capturing extinct things:

      unicorns

hands on my body

                    salvation

If I take another BuzzFeed quiz that says
my spirit poet is Sylvia Plath, I'll go back
in time & befriend her, stroke her hair
& kiss her mouth deeply in hopes that the oven
never turns on—

Violin

For Li-na

My first was a strumming thing
Broken strings
Chin rest scraped from misuse
You would cock my head
with your lean hands
position the bow against
the center bout
slow weave
I'd slide the horse-haired
rod a man's tongue
the strings would flick
You wanted me to learn
Verdi & I wanted to
work it like a fiddle
like Charles Ingalls
my blue collar body
aching to lick the rib
pounce the f-hole
twang the saddle
You said I had no
finesse, that it was about
love making & if I
couldn't learn to do it
on an instrument, I'd never
do it right. Last night
I fucked all night & yet
my fingers were positioned

as you once taught me
my ring finger on the G
& how that instrument
moaned—it crooned
you would've been proud
you would've given me
a standing ovation—

On Finding Out that Eartha Kitt Engaged in a Threesome with James Dean & Paul Newman

I can't for the life of me imagine
such splendor
it is said that Eartha labeled it the most
"celestial experience"
Brown buds & pink dicks
& I believe it. I tell Christina
that in times of peace my body
craves women,
but in times of war, upheaval, deep chaos; only
two men would do—She tells me
I am on to something
& I imagine the war that led Eartha
to that kind of lovely tangled
mess, how her body made them bend.
How they were rope,
snake & rod. How they worshipped her.
Paul's blue eyes piercing & deliberate
making wildfire   there—
& how James' pretty mouth hummed
an indulgent vacuum
against her folds. I tell you there has been
war all around me for months now.
I fear the future, a post-apocalyptic
scene out of a movie that has yet to be
made. I tell my body: easy lady, we're in
a pandemic, you're asking for too much.
& still the news each day tells me unauthorized

troops will be headed to my city
& my vote will get lost somewhere between
my home & whatever office deems it real.
I am lethargic in my activism, I have been lulled
into inertia, all I do is touch
myself with more than four hands; I live for
my next orgasm, I dream in twos.
On my knees in front of my altar
I pray to Eartha for her quick wit, her fine ass
body, her opportunities; so I may lose all sense
while the tear gas is set loose, while the dictator
reigns—fuck I am only human & all I want is
to feel   safe

We Started with Madness & Ended in Car Washes

For Elma's Heart Circle & Nipsey

We are a rebellion
a cuckoo clock that never stops
We make warfare   daily
& if I could call us anything
I'd call us   poem

Yesterday I said madness
& you said everything else
cause we're our own language
our own hands reaching
for something familiar
                    in the dark

We were meant to be
our own little kingdom
with big mouths & smart
comments. We open wide
& it's a wormhole—

We suck in & spit out
We make plans & find trouble
We say I love you & we mean
                    thank you

I woke up wanting to say
one true thing: friendship

is the only country whose
sovereignty I recognize

People underestimate us
we're only shy   not unambitious

We are gonna make gazillions
off of   automated
          car washes
in Hunts Point & Riverdale

It's going to slap the madness
out of us, when we jet set
to the Riviera or St. Barts or
City Island—that dreamy place
                    off the coast of the Bronx—

I swoon at the sight of us
I rattle
My whole heart a dying dwarf
                    till you—

MUSE FOUND IN A COLONIZED BODY

IX.

When I am hungry I eat
with my eyes
first. So much so that by the time
everyone has said grace
& is digging in, I am
full. I am the same
with love. & sometimes
I am the same with a great
idea. & these two things
might seem mutually
exclusive
but they are not—all love
starts off as a great idea
& all heartbreak is due to
poor execution.

Muse Found on Tinder

Your personal statement: KEEP IT SIMPLE, STUPID!
& I swipe because of your eyes   two Neptunes
& you write to me first: *You're so fucking gorgeous, the things I'd do to you—*
& I obsess over your taut body, tight muscles over a Viking's skeleton.

      & before we've even met I've written
      three poems   & have come   twice

& I need to
see you
touch you
because when water is this free you keep the faucet running

      & my sister warns me about: white boys

they will treat us
      like our daddies do
          constant   *abandonment*

& I ignore her
because
I am so fucking gorgeous
    & the things you'd do to me—

& when we meet I realize we're each other's fetish
& when we meet I am already contemplating the door
in the back of my mind
I am terrified of a microaggression

              in bed   naked
I'll be forced to   remain silent
After all   I am a coward

& I need you to be this way,   a man
                    that stays—

Everything Is Crumbling

so I looked up my birth chart
I needed a reminder for why
I always wanna run away from
stability—being a Leo in sign &
rising can't compete with my
Gemini moon, how it becomes
bored at the slightest sense
of habitual dress up, how it fears
being a fraud & my Venus
how it resides in Cancer & its 7th
house of perpetual falling—
how I might die falling off cliffs,
down stairs, in love—how if
I look at someone & wish: be
mine, what I mean is: tell me
I'm worthy. How all I really want
is to be a Pisces moon like my
mother, whose madness is a
cursive M pinned to the soles
of her feet. How she steps off
chairs & buildings & trees &
never falls. How she floats—
a star dangling—a spore,
an albatross strewing
against a periwinkle blue—

MUSE FOUND IN A COLONIZED BODY

X.

How useless I must be
This colonized thing

generations removed from
the conquistador & the slave

How I barely remember
my native tongue   & how

the last time I felt as
regal as a queen I was in

someone's bed naked & still
starving as I picked their meat

from my teeth. I sometimes dare to
take what is not mine   taking

might be too tender of a word,
I think I mean   I might kill
for what I think I love—

& part of forgiveness is to forgive
yourself & the ancestors that live inside
                    of you.

Lately, I've been dreaming of destroying
everything I've built. Taking my life between
my fingers like a plum & squeezing until

there is nothing. I don't know whether
this is my ancestor the slave   feeling

so lost & trapped that the only option
is to burn his world down   or

my ancestor who landed en el Caribe
& not knowing the names for things

named them all after his own image

I want to believe that I am better than
who I was in my last life I want to

believe that I am better than who
I've been in this one—

Notes on Self-Care

For Hikmet & Girmay

what better way to forget that the world is burning
than by imagining me in London Town with

Idris & his Luther wool coat with its deep
pockets where both my hands fit

as he walks me to his flat
& the décor is ridiculous: French chic

with some touches of Kentucky country
but it's my fantasy & there's no room for black leather

couches or 70-inch TVs—no bachelor's Shangri-La here
No beer in the fridge, only rows & rows of vintage Bordeaux

I chase Idris across my forehead
whirling into bed with him like a wrecking ball

envisioning his scruff face
against my neck, his beard

better than any exfoliator I've ever owned

his languid fingers like rakes
against my plump body

& he loves my poems—

all of him, his 40 trillion cells
at attention to every stanza I write

& what better way to live than to desire this way?
& this is not escapism   it's survival—

One day, this earth will rot
or worse   be made good

& there will be no need
for this sort of daydreaming

One day, this earth will be good
or worse   we'll be good

& Idris will be a faint taste of something I once
wanted like trees shedding against a November sky

I'll sit down to write a poem
about the time I fantasized I made love to Idris Elba

not remembering how in my sorrow he held
me like one of my metaphors

between his fingers
as though my poems were just delusions

foliage falling to the earth routine & dying

thin as rice paper

tender as paper cranes—

Imagining Him Running at the Sight of Deer

For Roberto Carlos Garcia

I was not there, but she tells me the story over & over
how after spotting a mob of deer he ran like someone
who is afraid to become the other becoming, the sound
an animal makes all guttural, bottomless & rooted. He
who feeds me joy & sorrow equally, with golden tongue
& eyes so bright I imagine stars once living in the hollow
sockets of his caramel face. & let's be clear, he ran
from deer, because he knows that beautiful doesn't always
equal tame & that gentle things are the ones that risk it all—

Which is to say, if deer could talk, they will tell you something
about wanting to kill a thing & about being killed.
& we oblige. We kill them for sport & with great
carelessness—& we do each other the same. So he ran from
deer, because maybe he understands that one day the targeted
animal will fight back. It will straighten out his long neck like
a heron & his eyes will become wild & this is what being hunted
does to a man, I mean deer, I mean any animal on this earth.
We live & we die, what happens in between is not up to fate,
but something more complex—

Say mystery
Say the lover's soft back in moonlight
Say fear
Say the smell of honeysuckle in a barren field
Say hunger

& I say run   run

It's the only thing our body does well enough

good enough   to stay alive—

I Was Wrong; Running Doesn't Save Us

once at eight years old I nearly gave myself a concussion running
my mother would braid my hair & wrap the ends in the heaviest
hair ties with the biggest colorful glass balls, they were lethal; as
was my running game—I was a child after all, all full of joy &
fury, all bubble gum & smart mouth, my legs were thunder, my
heart that of a horse. Later as I got older, running became something
I did to be thin, I would run on the treadmill & feel so beautiful
after a 3-mile run; the experts say endorphins, I say it was the only
way I knew to stay connected to my ancestors. I wonder if that was
what Ahmaud was doing that day—communing with those that
came before? Were they training him for the same situation he found
himself in that afternoon; running for his life—

white men with guns as
jury, white men where
killing is their favorite sport

Muse Found in a Cracked Spine

For Freddie & so on . . .

I want to make
this poem so
pretty, so thin,
so white; a spine.
I can do that.
Been writing
it in all my
different
incarnations
for over 400
years. This poem
about another
dead Black man.
This one will be
different, because
this one is about
my own
shortcomings.
I've wasted years
& have not
produced
one solider for
the cause. While
my enemies
are rabbits.
I've been barren.
Tonight I'm

gonna make
babies—
I have nothing
to give this
war apart from
bodies.
Bodies that will
die. Bodies that
will run.
Precious brown
bodies that can
take a beating.
Bodies, bodies, bodies.
Bodies that will
reproduce
more bodies
more bodies
bodies with
a poet's tongue
& baller's hands
& Basquiat's eye,
a surgeon's brain
a gangbanger's
heart.
Bodies is what
I am giving
this world; because
the winner will be
the one that is
willing to sacrifice
their children—

MUSE FOUND IN A COLONIZED BODY

XI.

This way
      I am colonized,   used
as a   commodity to a thankless master

I started out as a   servant because I knew
      no better.

Today I am a city, with a hospital
& a police force, a fire department too
so I can put myself out—

A Brief Meditation on Breath

i have diver's lungs from holding my
breath for so long. i promise you
i am not trying to break a record
sometimes i just forget to
exhale. my shoulders held tightly
near my neck, i am a ball of tense
living, a tumbleweed with steel-toed
boots. i can't remember the last time
i felt light as dandelion. i can't remember
the last time i took the sweetness in
& my diaphragm expanded into song.
they tell me breathing is everything,
meaning if i breathe right i can live to be
ancient. i'll grow a soft furry tail or be
telekinetic something powerful enough
to heal the world. i swear i thought
the last time i'd think of death with breath
was that balmy day in july when the cops
became a raging fire & sucked the breath
out of Garner; but yesterday i walked
38 blocks to my father's house with a mask
over my nose & mouth, the sweat dripping
off my chin only to get caught in fabric & pool up
like rain. & i inhaled small spurts of me, little
particles of my dna. i took into body my own self
& thought i'd die from so much exposure
to my own bereavement—they're saying
this virus takes your breath away, not

like a mother's love or like a good kiss
from your lover's soft mouth but like the police
it can kill you fast or slow: dealer's choice.
a pallbearer carrying your body without a casket.
they say it's so contagious it could be quite
breathtaking. so persistent it might as well
be breathing   down your neck—

Still

when you
read this
Trump might
still be in
office
& I'll
still be
falling
in love
with
wasteful
things
A dream
is only
a dream
if you
don't
take any
action be
still as a
sloth or
a wounded
animal
Still is the
root of lie
or lovely
Still there
is always

tomorrow
another
president
another
love
another
dream
subdued &
motionless
I once
saw 1000
flying fish
skating across
an endless
sea &
still
that was
not enough—

Muse Found in Magical Realism

She was born with lace gloves on.
It was a miracle.
Her hands were light   & everything
she touched turned to something
else.

It was a problem   clearly,
like when she learned to walk & went
about the house turning the furniture
into dolls. Porcelain everywhere—

Let's not even talk about her father's
face, the first time she touched his cheek
it was a tree, it offered her   shade
from the summer's heat.

Imagine when she learned how to kiss
she was fascinated by lips & reached for them.
Her first love sported an elephant's trunk
her second an owl's boney beak.

I want to say that at some point she
learned to control it, that when lonely
she would walk out into the city streets
touch a street lamp & a lover would appear

his beard perfect for touching. But she
was never able to, else he'd become another

thing.   Her ability grew unapologetic
she touched her breasts once & they grew
two sizes with orchid faces.

& did I mention she never mastered the art
of love   fickle thing, how could she?
When everything she desired always turned
out to be   different.

Towards the end, she took off the gloves
to feel the world & it turned into a pile of
clovers. Having lost everything she touched
her own body   & became cattle
she ate the world   ate it all—

A C K N O W L E D G M E N T S

To those who tether me to this world. Thank you. I love you: Eric De Silva, Maritza Rodriguez, Hector B. Montilla, Maritza Montilla, Carlos Montilla, Hector M. Montilla, Jaylin Montilla, Jonah Montilla, Destiny Montilla, Iris Montilla-Afriye, William Afriye, Christopher Mitchell, Manny Rodriguez, Cary Rodriguez, Andrew Rodriguez, & my California fam who are a tribe of light & love that hold me: Mel, Tania, Kimmy, & all the babies big & small. To those who give me wings, my work would not be what it is without you: Kathy Engel, Ella Engel-Snow, Jaja Engel-Snow, Jonathan Snow, Cheryl Boyce Taylor, Alexis Deveaux, Mahogany L. Browne, Denice Frohman, Christina Olivares, Ricky Maldonado, Sheila Maldonado, Peggy Robles-Alvarado, Carina Del Valle Schorske, Diana Marie Delgado, Aracelis Girmay, John Murillo, Rachel Eliza Griffiths, Ross Gay, Patrick Rosal, Darla Himeles, Peter Kirn, Sean Morrissey, & Roberto Carlos Garcia. My mentors, co-conspirators, & allies: Natalie Diaz, Anne Marie Macari, Gerald Stern, Michael Waters, Mihaela Moscaliuc, Judith Vollmer, Evie Shockley, Willie Perdomo, Joan Larkin, Patricia Smith, Marwa Helal, Elisabet Velasquez, Elizabeth Acevedo, Nicole Sealy, Malcom Friend, Gabriel Ramirez, Rosebud Ben Oni, Grisel Y. Acosta, Vincent Toro, Lupe Mendez, Seema Reza, Ellen Hagen, LeConte Dill, E.J. Antonio, Caits Meissner, Cheryl Clarke, & JP Howard. Thank you also to those who have been more than co-workers, those that help me survive the day-to-day grind: Cindia Quintana, Kojo Ahenkorah, Sashell Kelly, Demetrius Lemons, Michael Lee, Janette Figueroa, Roxanna Gonzalez, Kerry Ann Williams, Oghale Jituboh, & Clelia Mogolofsky. I am nothing without the following crews, institutions, & spaces that hold & have held me: Elma's Heart Circle, Enclave Habitat, Cave Canem, Women Writers in Bloom, Kundiman, Letras Latinas, & CantoMundo. Martha Rhodes, Ryan Murphy, & the entire Four Way Books family, you took a chance on this book, you helped usher it into the world, my deep gratitude to you. I will miss people, I have missed people, but know that you're never too far from my mind & that we are all so interconnected I wouldn't be me, these poems wouldn't be here without you too. Lastly, to my many ancestors whose names are bright stars on my tongue, thank you for holding me & strengthening me from the other world: Luisa, Martin, Leopoldo, Reina & so on—

I'd like to acknowledge as well the following publications for giving my poems from this collection a home:

Academy of American Poets, *Poem-A-Day*; *The Acentos Review*; *Apogee Journal*; *Best of American Poetry, 2021*; *Best of American Poetry Blog*; *Black Poets Speak Out Anthology*; *The Breakbeat Poets Vol. 4: LatiNext Anthology*; Center for Book Arts; *Chicago Quarterly Review*; *Choice Words: Writers on Abortion*; *Colorado Review*; *Connotation Press*; *Divine Feminist: An Anthology of Poetry & Art by Womxn & Non-Binary Folx*; *Gulf Coast*; *Mistake House Magazine*; *Origins Journal*; *Pittsburg Poetry Review*; *Prairie Schooner*; Split This Rock, & *Tribes*.

ABOUT THE AUTHOR

Yesenia Montilla is an Afro-Latina poet and a daughter of immigrants. She received her MFA from Drew University in Poetry and Poetry in translation. She is a CantoMundo graduate fellow and a 2020 NYFA fellow. Her work has been published in the Academy of American Poets Poem-a-Day, *Prairie Schooner*, *Gulf Coast*, and in *Best of American Poetry 2020*. Her first collection *The Pink Box* is published by Willow Books and was longlisted for a PEN award. *Muse Found in a Colonized Body* is her second collection. She lives in Harlem, NY.

Publication of this book was made possible by grants and donations. We are also grateful to those individuals who participated in our 2021 Build a Book Program. They are:

Anonymous (16), Maggie Anderson, Susan Kay Anderson, Kristina Andersson, Kate Angus, Kathy Aponick, Sarah Audsley, Jean Ball, Sally Ball, Clayre Benzadón, Greg Blaine, Laurel Blossom, adam bohannon, Betsy Bonner, Lee Briccetti, Joan Bright, Jane Martha Brox, Susan Buttenwieser, Anthony Cappo, Carla and Steven Carlson, Paul and Brandy Carlson, Renee Carlson, Alice Christian, Karen Rhodes Clarke, Mari Coates, Jane Cooper, Ellen Cosgrove, Peter Coyote, Robin Davidson, Kwame Dawes, Michael Anna de Armas, Brian Komei Dempster, Renko and Stuart Dempster, Matthew DeNichilo, Rosalynde Vas Dias, Kent Dixon, Patrick Donnelly, Lynn Emanuel, Blas Falconer, Elliot Figman, Jennifer Franklin, Helen Fremont and Donna Thagard, Gabriel Fried, John Gallaher, Reginald Gibbons, Jason Gifford, Jean and Jay Glassman, Dorothy Tapper Goldman, Sarah Gorham and Jeffrey Skinner, Lauri Grossman, Julia Guez, Sarah Gund, Naomi Guttman and Jonathan Mead, Kimiko Hahn, Mary Stewart Hammond, Beth Harrison, Jeffrey Harrison, Melanie S. Hatter, Tom Healy and Fred Hochberg, K.T. Herr, Karen Hildebrand, Joel Hinman, Deming Holleran, Lillian Howan, Thomas and Autumn Howard, Catherine Hoyser, Elizabeth Jackson, Jessica Jacobs and Nickole Brown, Christopher Johanson, Jen Just, Maeve Kinkead, Alexandra Knox, Lindsay and John Landes, Suzanne Langlois, Laura Lauth, Sydney Lea, David Lee and Jamila Trindle, Rodney Terich Leonard, Jen Levitt, Howard Levy, Owen Lewis, Matthew Lippman, Jennifer Litt, Karen Llagas, Sara London and Dean Albarelli, Clarissa Long, James Longenbach, Cynthia Lowen, Ralph and Mary Ann Lowen, Ricardo Maldonado, Myra Malkin, Jacquelyn Malone, Carrie Mar, Kathleen McCoy, Ellen McCulloch-Lovell, Lupe Mendez, David Miller, Josephine Miller, Nicki Moore, Guna Mundheim, Matthew Murphy and

Maura Rockcastle, Michael and Nancy Murphy, Myra Natter, Jay Baron
Nicorvo, Ashley Nissler, Kimberly Nunes, Rebecca and Daniel Okrent,
Robert Oldshue and Nina Calabresi, Kathleen Ossip, Judith Pacht, Cathy
McArthur Palermo, Marcia and Chris Pelletiere, Sam Perkins, Susan
Peters and Morgan Driscoll, Patrick Phillips, Robert Pinsky, Megan Pinto,
Connie Post, Kyle Potvin, Grace Prasad, Kevin Prufer, Alicia Jo Rabins,
Anna Duke Reach, Victoria Redel, Martha Rhodes, Paula Rhodes, Louise
Riemer, Sarah Santner, Amy Schiffman, Peter and Jill Schireson, Roni and
Richard Schotter, James and Nancy Shalek, Soraya Shalforoosh, Peggy
Shinner, Anita Soos, Donna Spruijt-Metz, Ann F. Stanford, Arlene Stang,
Page Hill Starzinger, Marina Stuart, Yerra Sugarman, Marjorie and Lew
Tesser, Eleanor Thomas, Tom Thompson and Miranda Field, James Tjoa,
Ellen Bryant Voigt, Connie Voisine, Moira Walsh, Ellen Dore Watson,
Calvin Wei, John Wender, Eleanor Wilner, Mary Wolf, and Pamela and
Kelly Yenser.